SCADA and ME

A Book for Children and Management

By
Robert M. Lee

Illustrated by
Jeff Haas

Copyright Robert M. Lee

Published by IT-Harvest Press, 2013
Birmingham, Michigan
www.ith-press.com

ISBN-13: 978-1491275122
ISBN-10: 149127512X

Printed in the United States

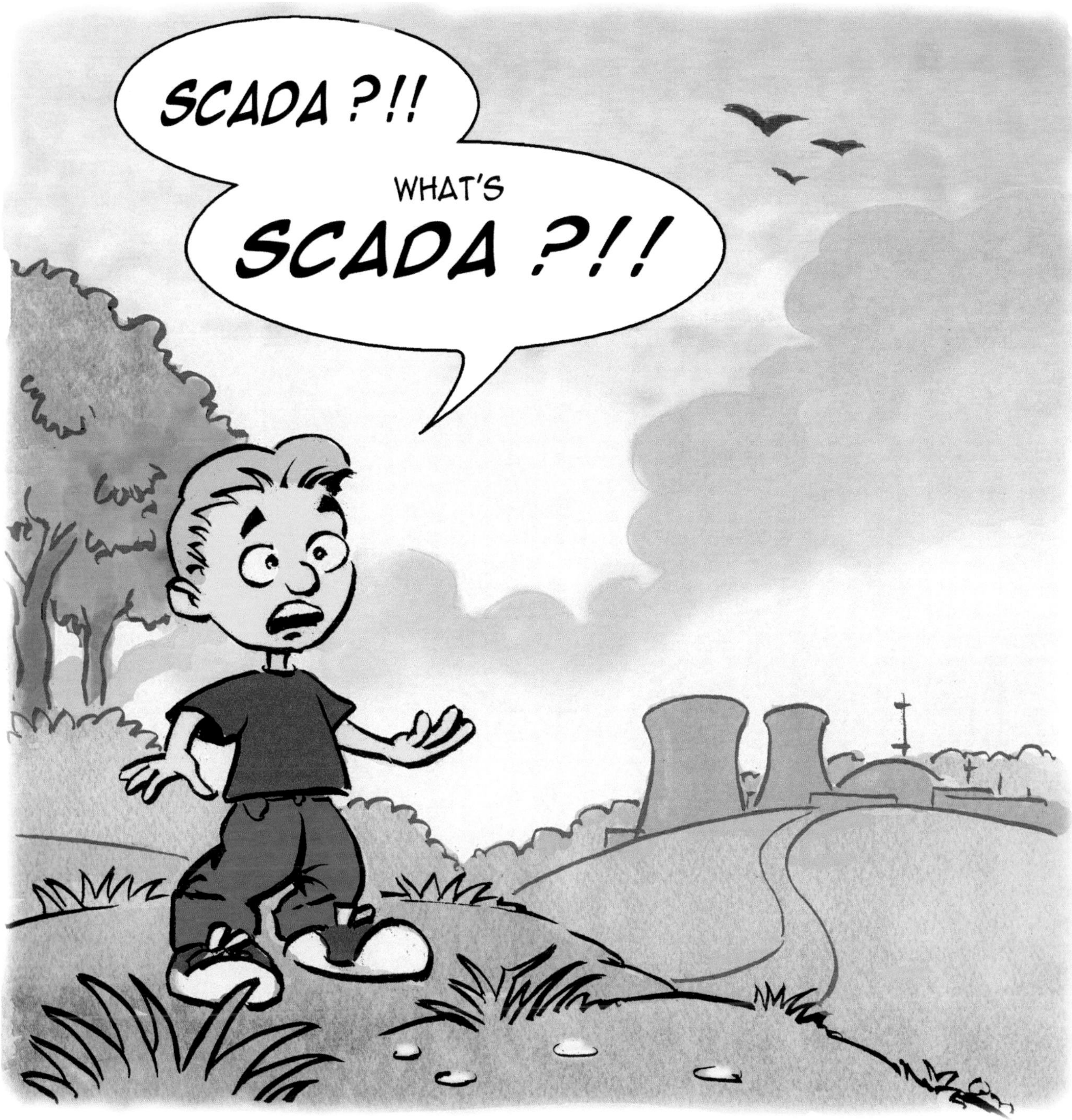
SCADA ?!!
WHAT'S
SCADA ?!!

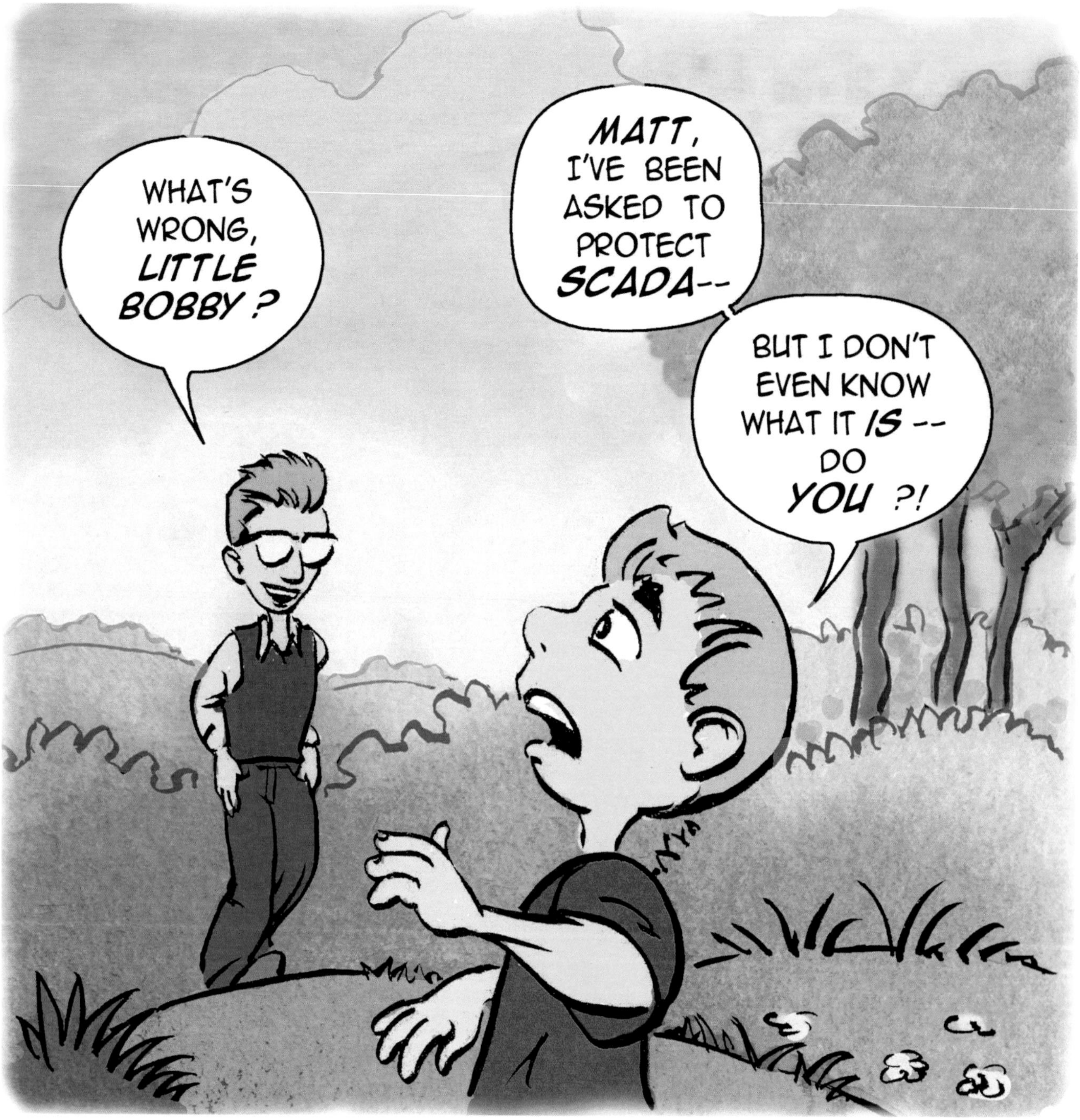
WHAT'S WRONG, LITTLE BOBBY ?
MATT, I'VE BEEN ASKED TO PROTECT SCADA--
BUT I DON'T EVEN KNOW WHAT IT IS -- DO YOU ?!

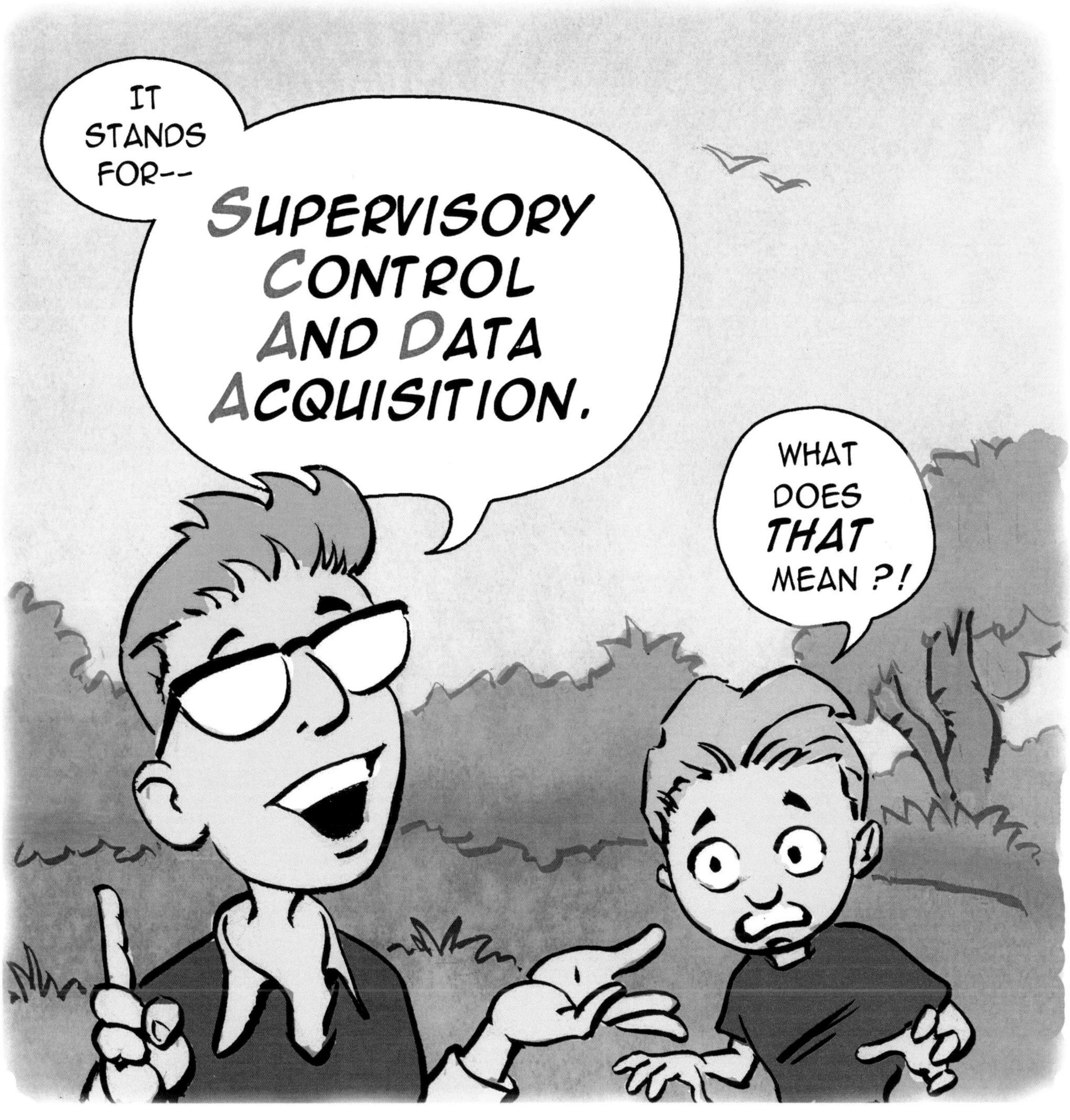
IT STANDS FOR--
SUPERVISORY CONTROL AND DATA ACQUISITION.
WHAT DOES THAT MEAN ?!

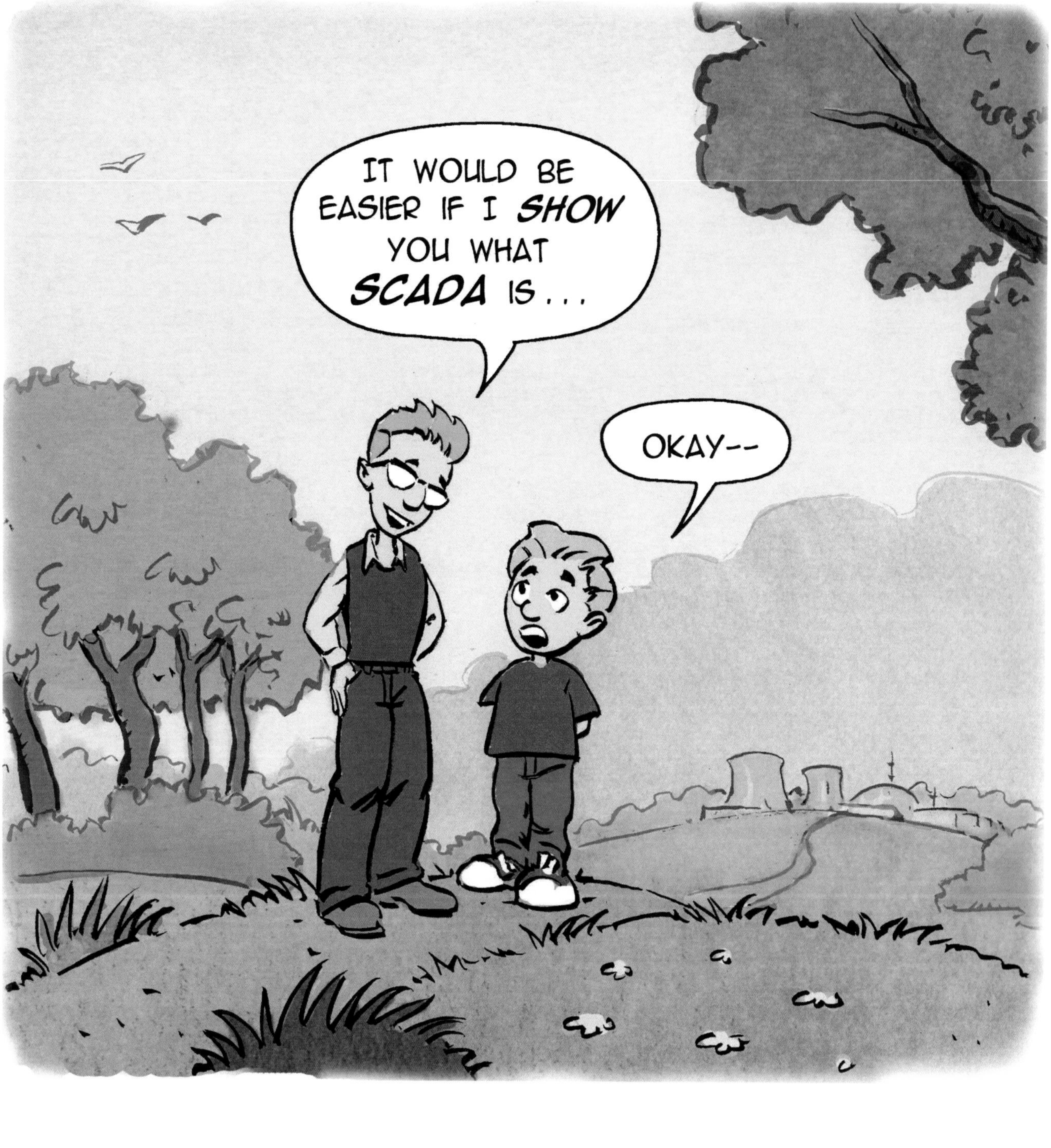
IT WOULD BE EASIER IF I *SHOW* YOU WHAT *SCADA* IS . . .
OKAY--

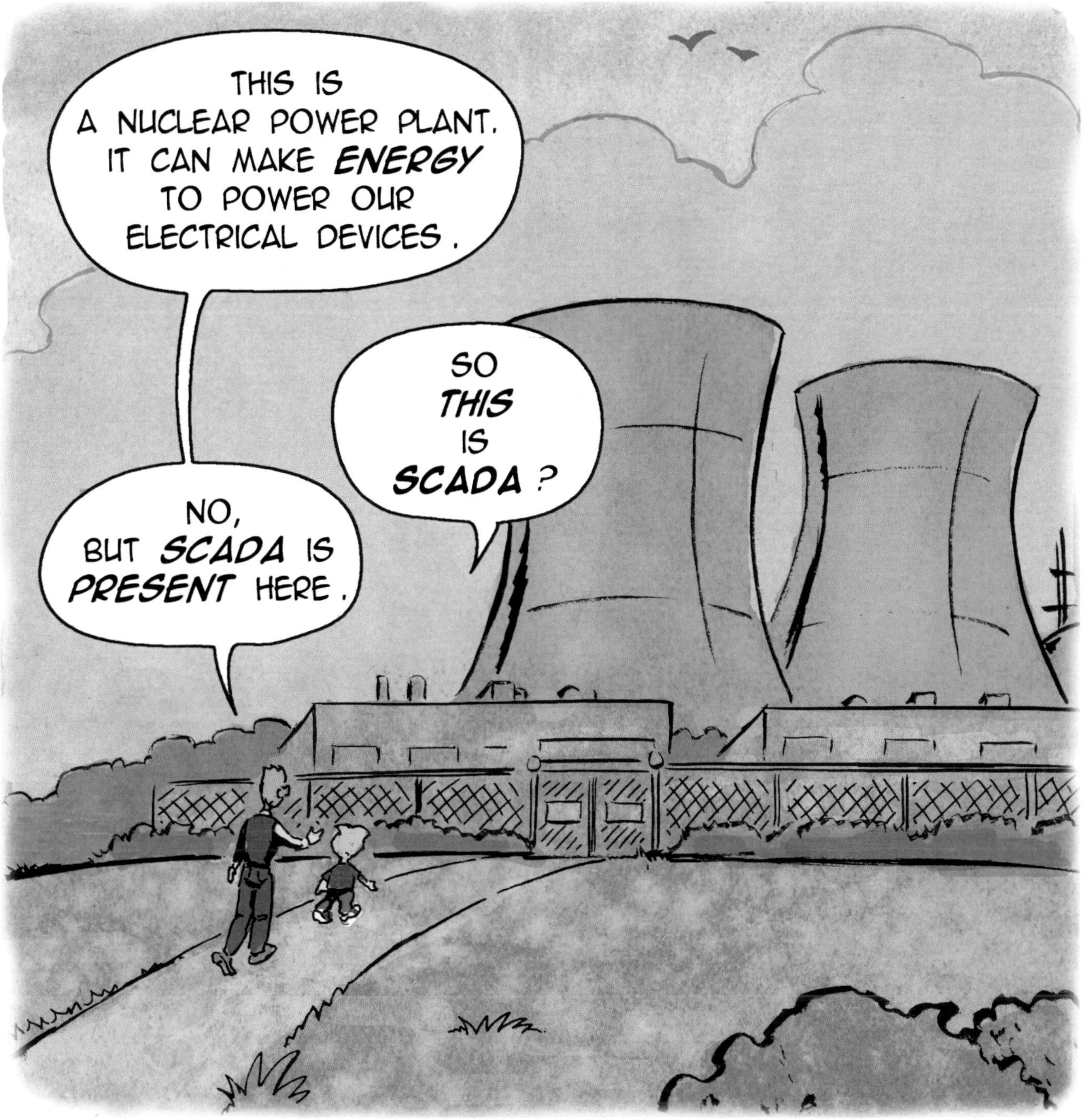
THIS IS A NUCLEAR POWER PLANT. IT CAN MAKE *ENERGY* TO POWER OUR ELECTRICAL DEVICES.
SO *THIS* IS *SCADA*?
NO, BUT *SCADA* IS *PRESENT* HERE.

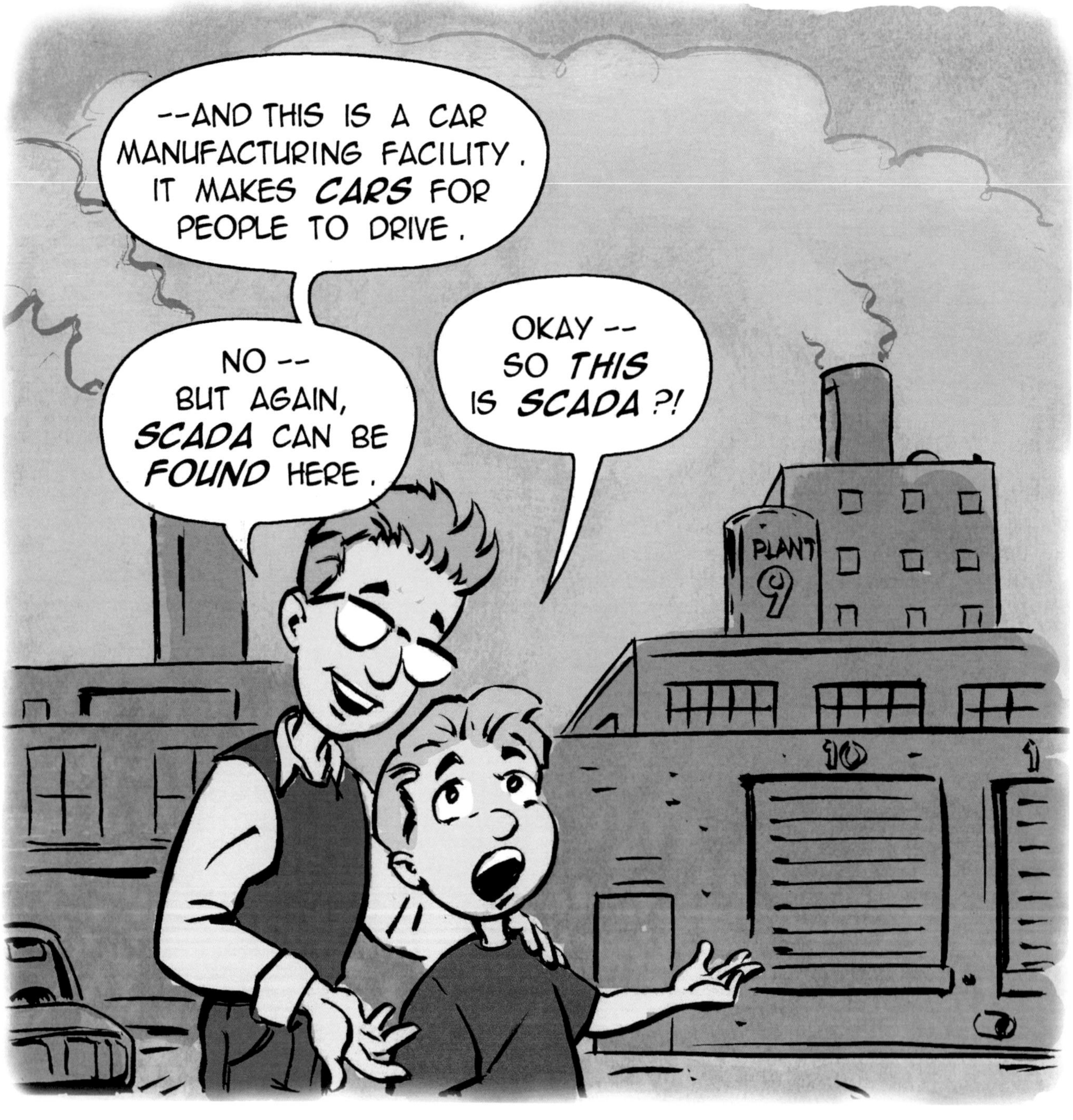
--AND THIS IS A CAR MANUFACTURING FACILITY. IT MAKES CARS FOR PEOPLE TO DRIVE.
OKAY -- SO THIS IS SCADA?!
NO -- BUT AGAIN, SCADA CAN BE FOUND HERE.
PLANT 9
10

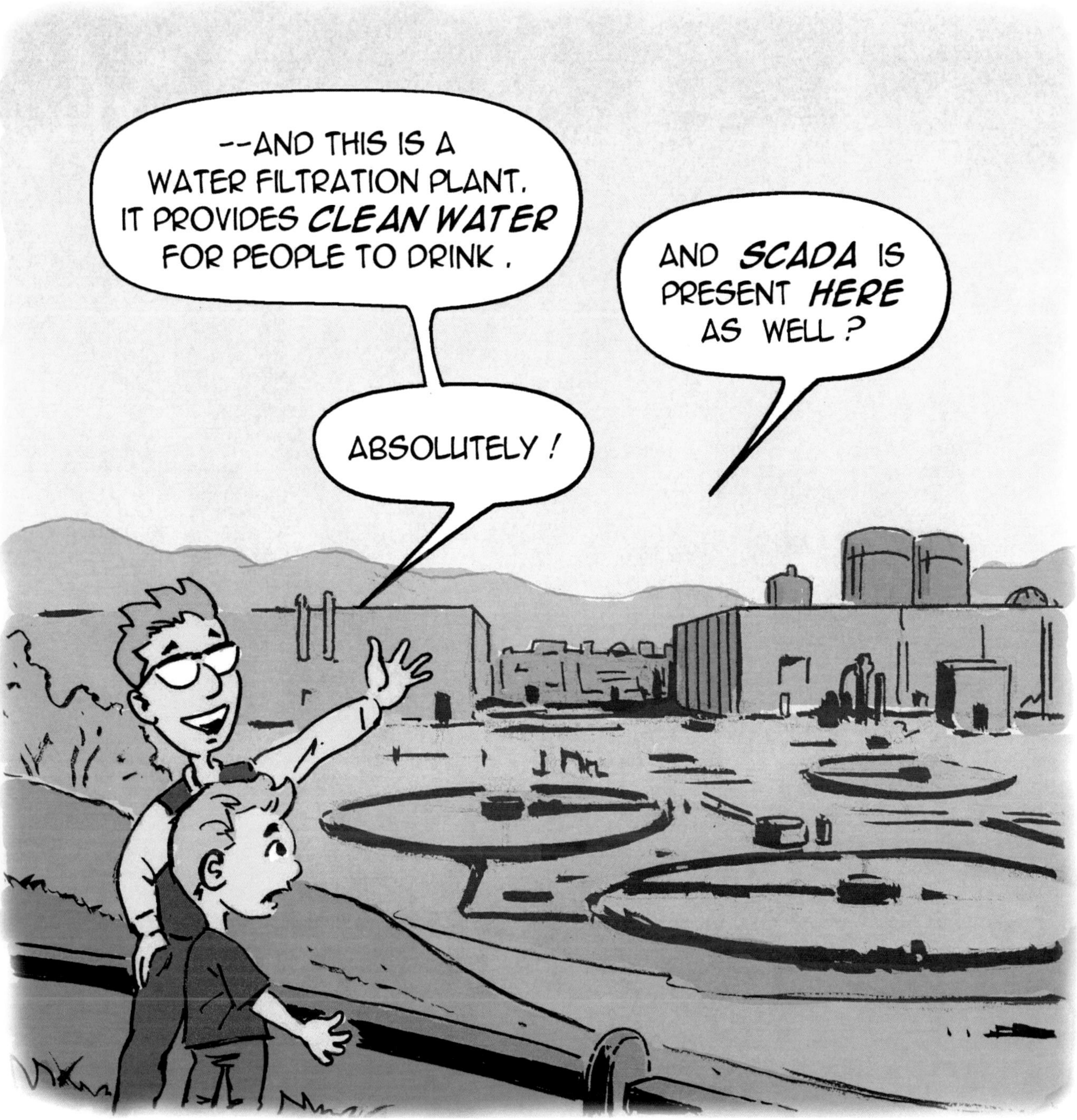
--AND THIS IS A WATER FILTRATION PLANT. IT PROVIDES CLEAN WATER FOR PEOPLE TO DRINK.
AND SCADA IS PRESENT HERE AS WELL?
ABSOLUTELY!

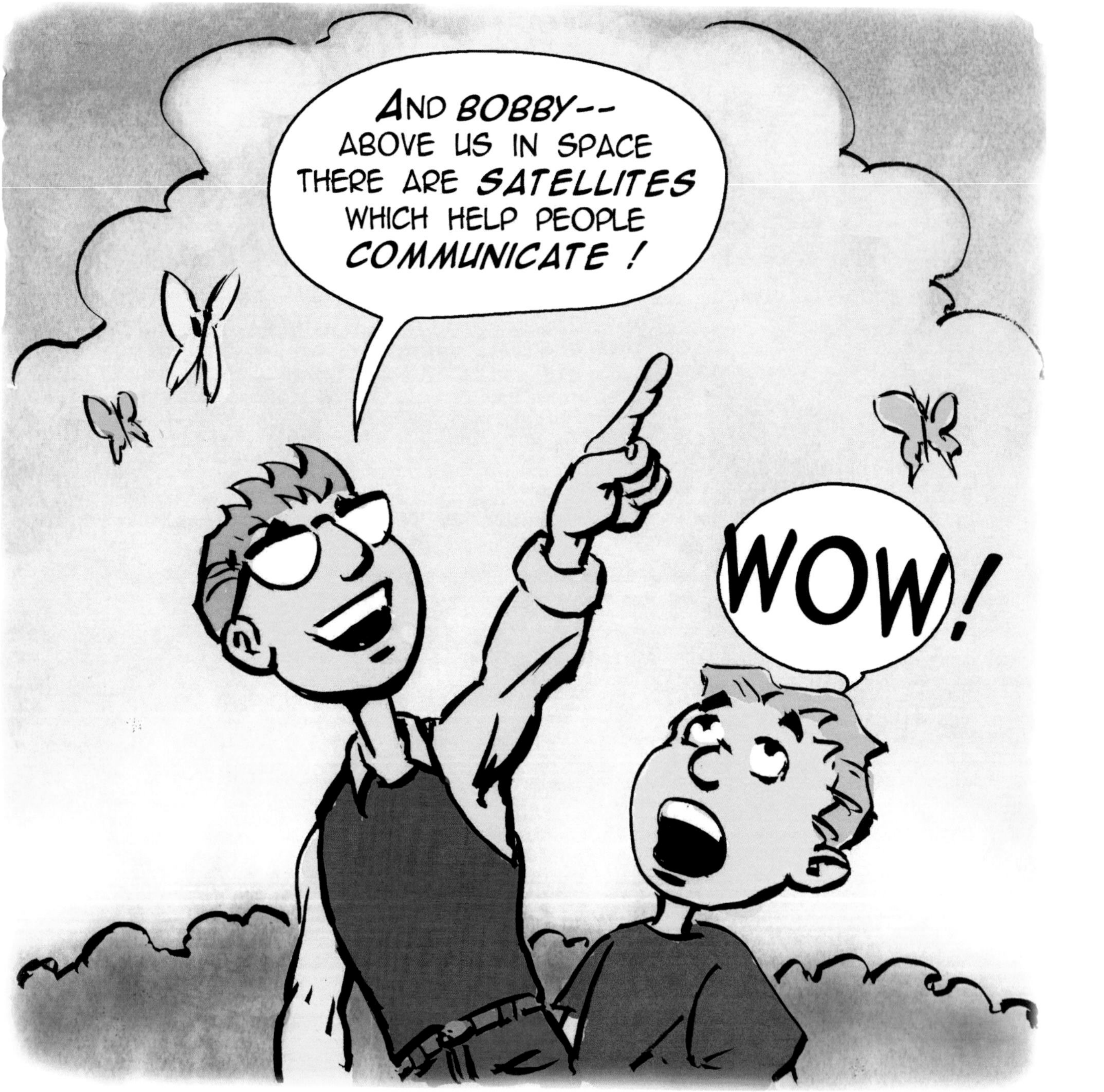
AND BOBBY-- ABOVE US IN SPACE THERE ARE SATELLITES WHICH HELP PEOPLE COMMUNICATE !
WOW!

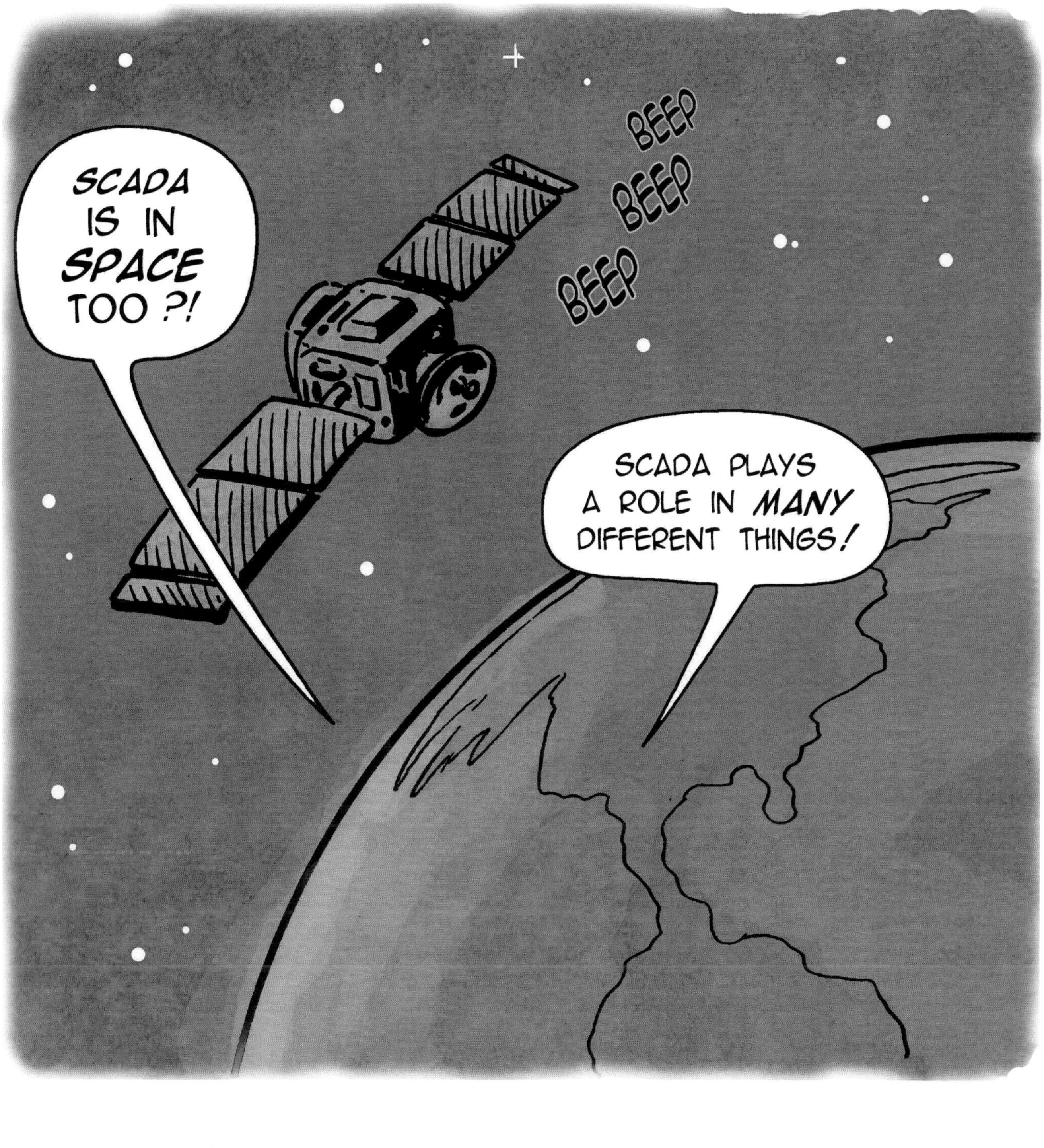
SCADA IS IN *SPACE* TOO ?!
BEEP BEEP BEEP
SCADA PLAYS A ROLE IN *MANY* DIFFERENT THINGS!

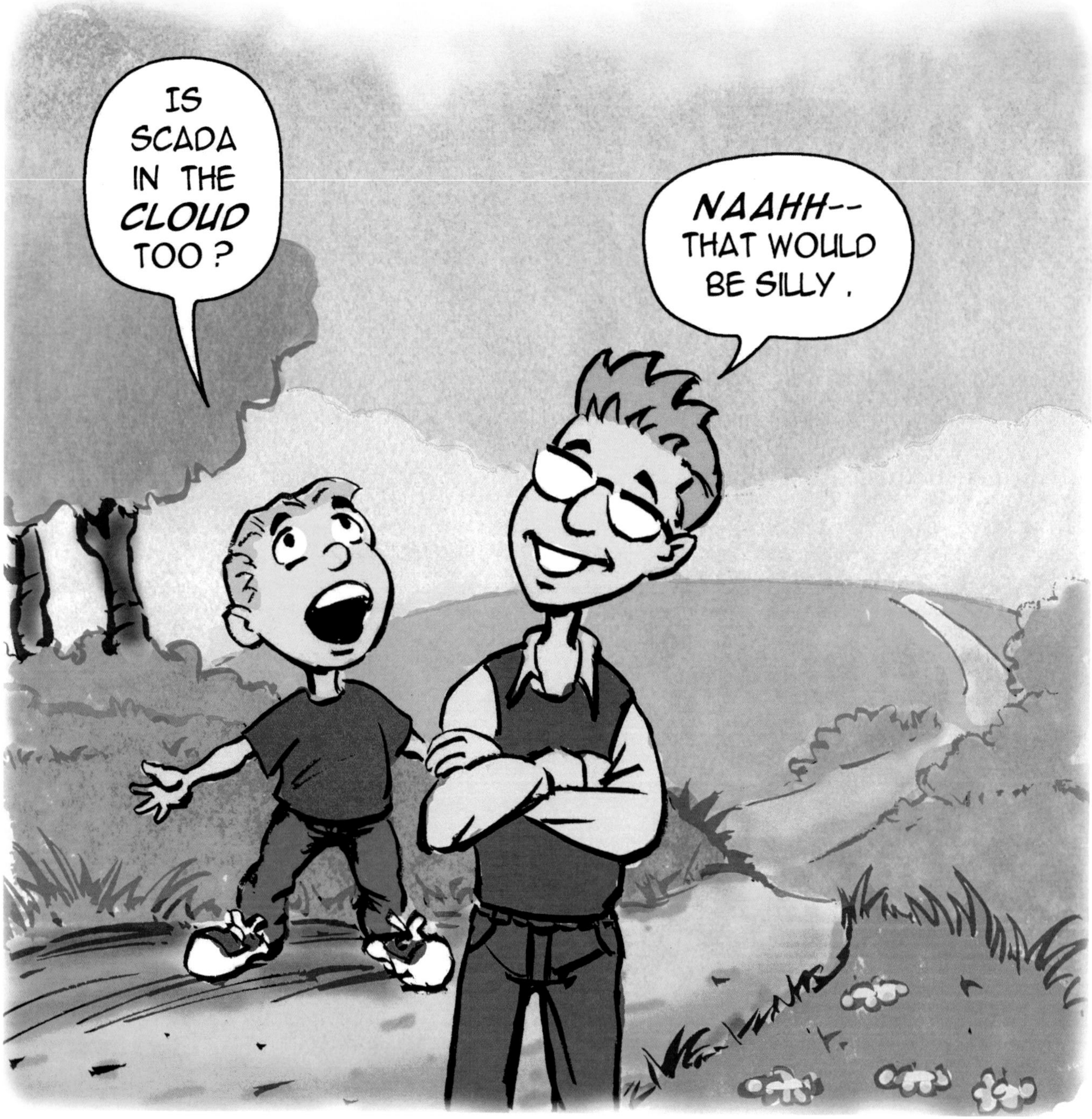

IS SCADA IN THE CLOUD TOO ?
NAAHH-- THAT WOULD BE SILLY .

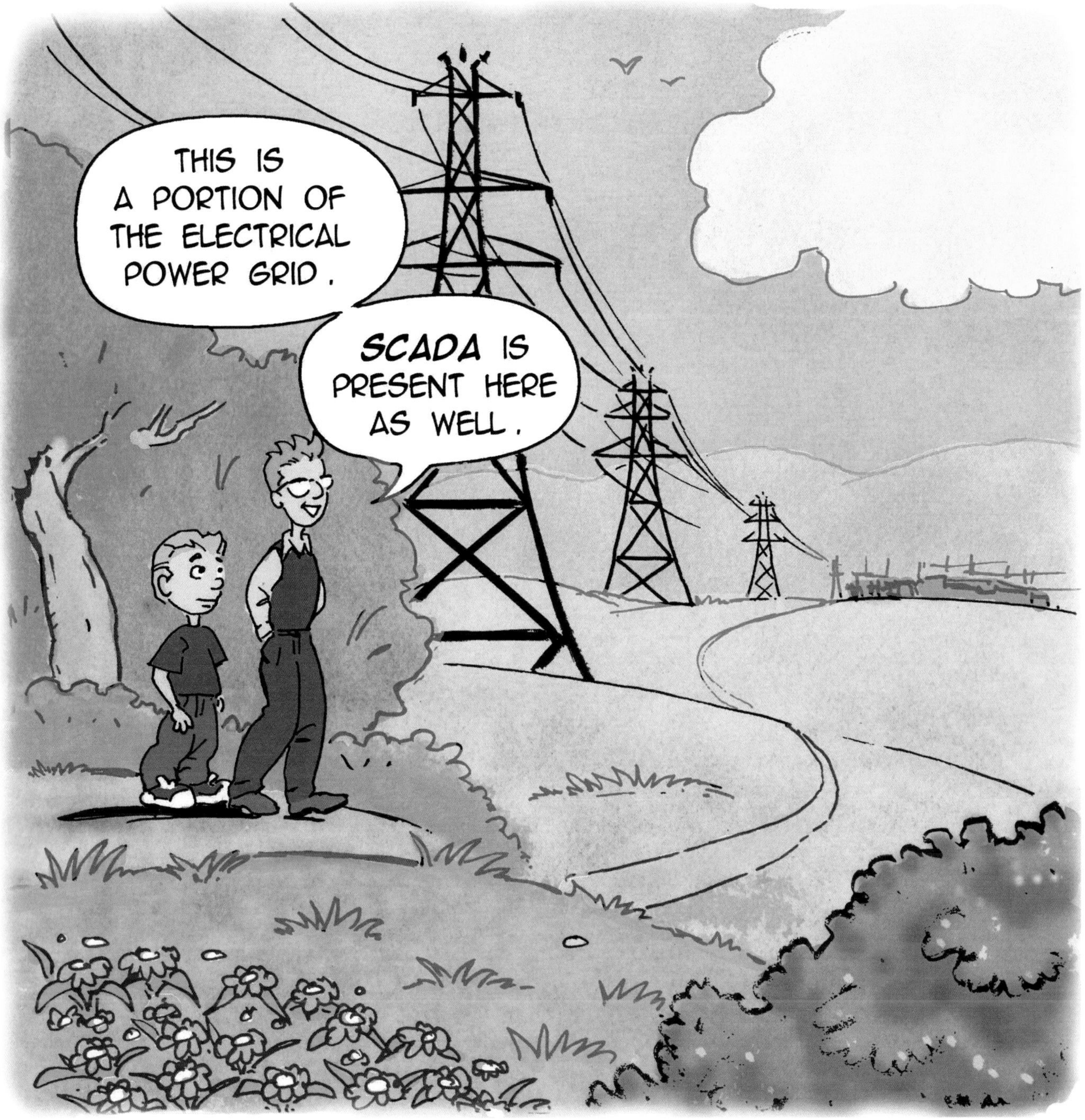
THIS IS A PORTION OF THE ELECTRICAL POWER GRID.
SCADA IS PRESENT HERE AS WELL.

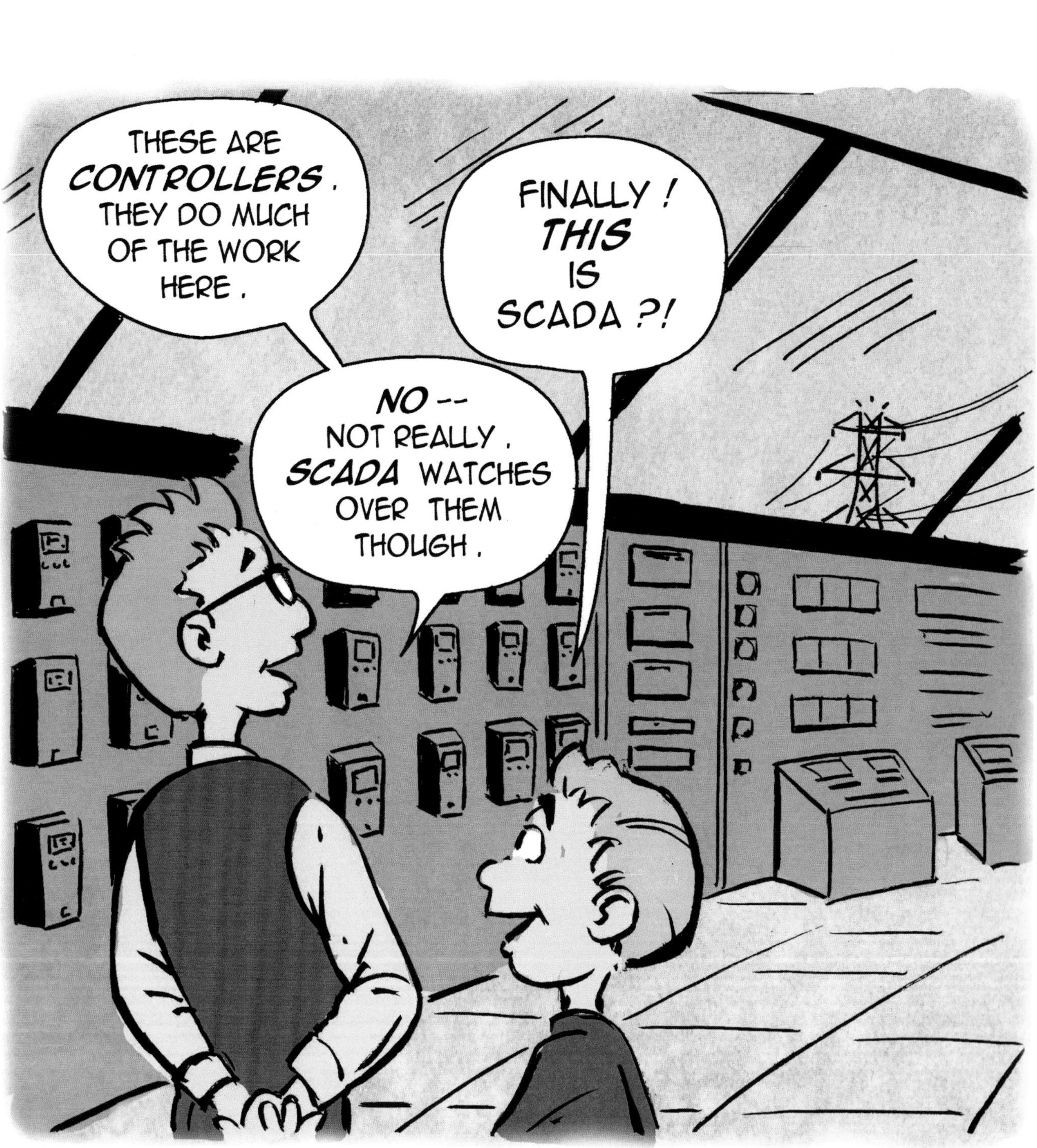
THESE ARE CONTROLLERS. THEY DO MUCH OF THE WORK HERE.
FINALLY! THIS IS SCADA?!
NO -- NOT REALLY. SCADA WATCHES OVER THEM THOUGH.

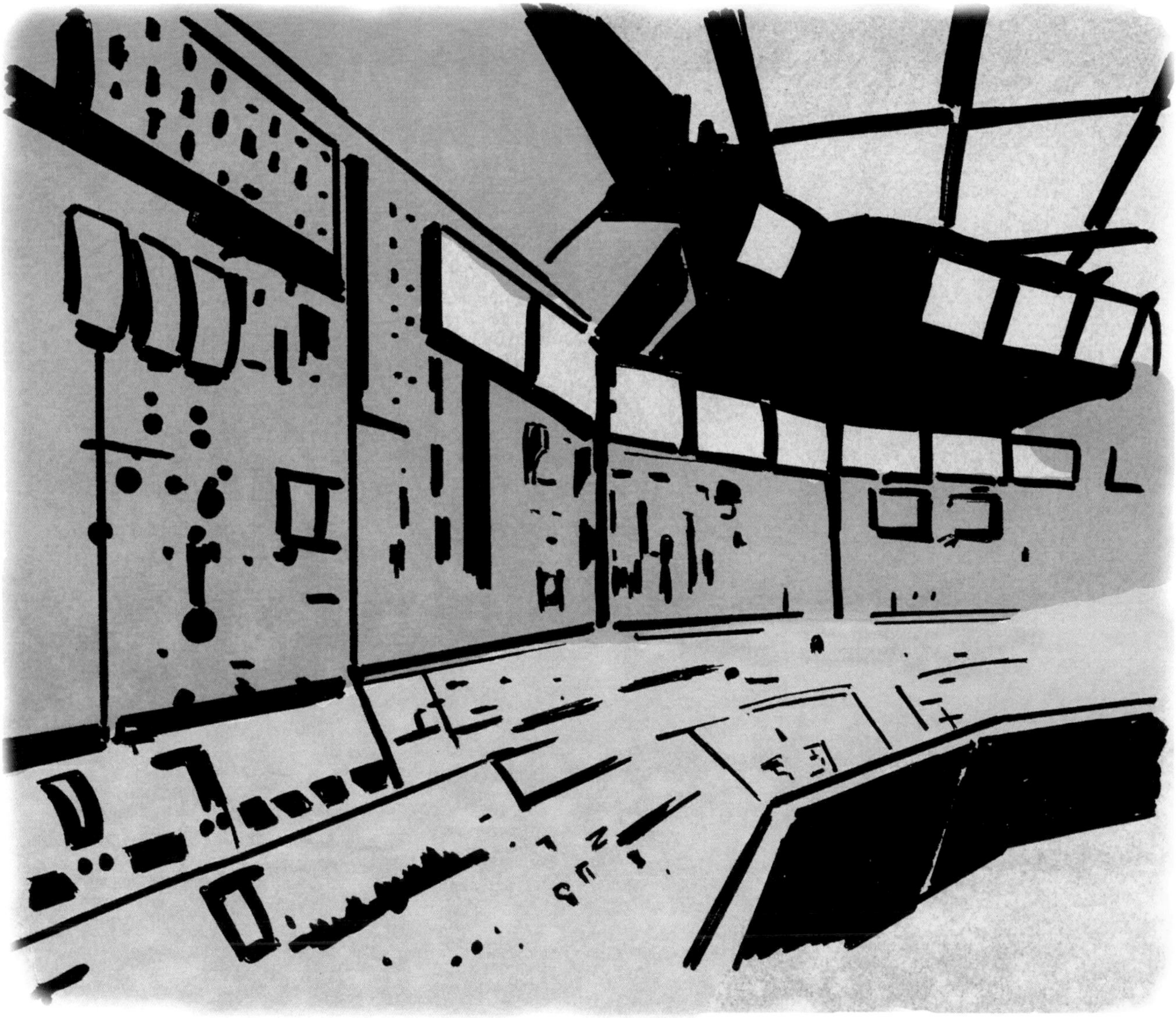

SCADA EXISTS ON COMPUTERS LIKE THIS. IT'S LIKE A BABYSITTER -- CONSTANTLY WATCHING AND GUIDING MANY CHILDREN. CHILDREN SUCH AS THE ***CONTROLLERS***.

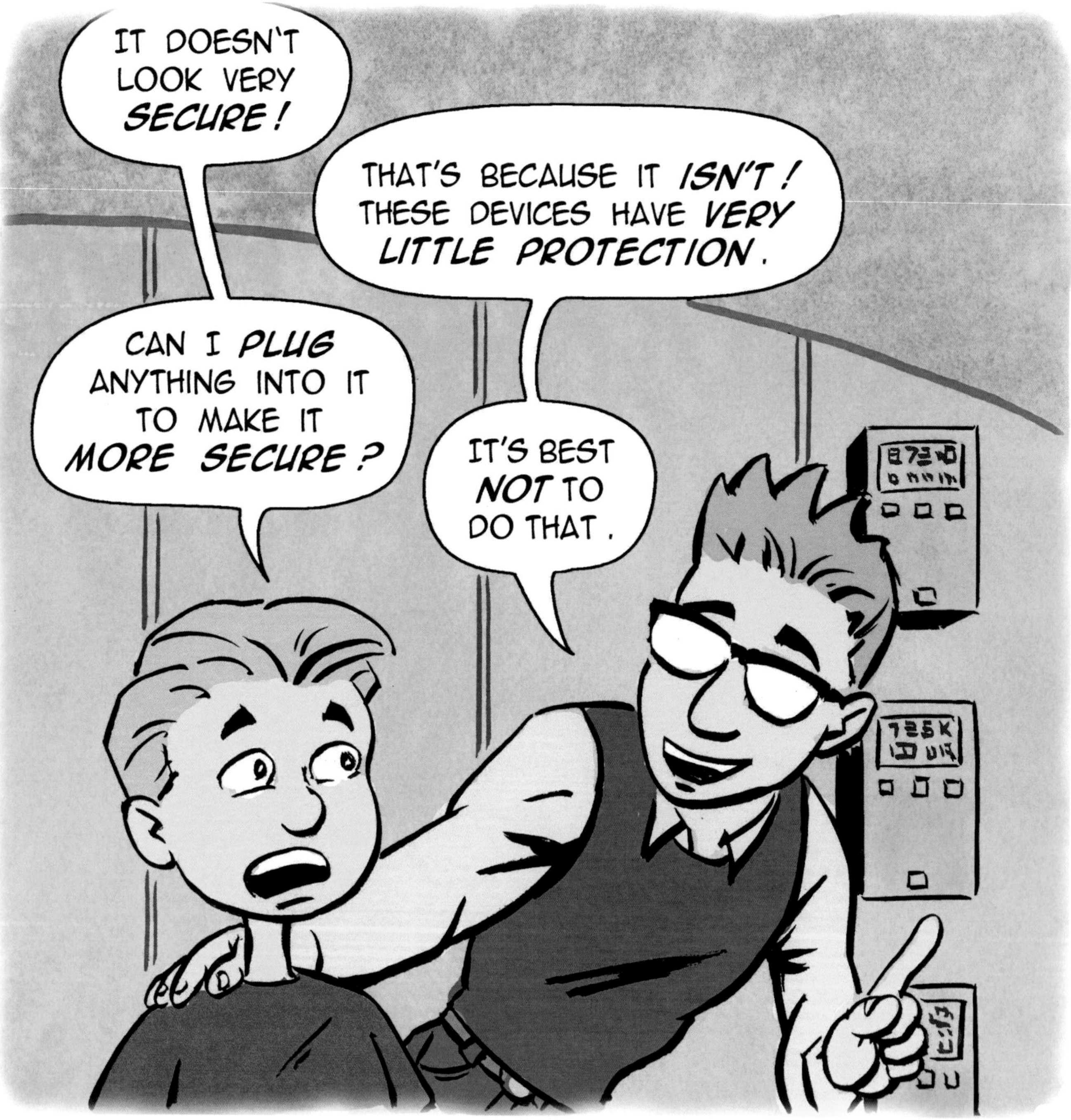
IT DOESN'T LOOK VERY *SECURE!*
THAT'S BECAUSE IT *ISN'T!* THESE DEVICES HAVE *VERY LITTLE PROTECTION.*
CAN I *PLUG* ANYTHING INTO IT TO MAKE IT *MORE SECURE?*
IT'S BEST *NOT* TO DO THAT.

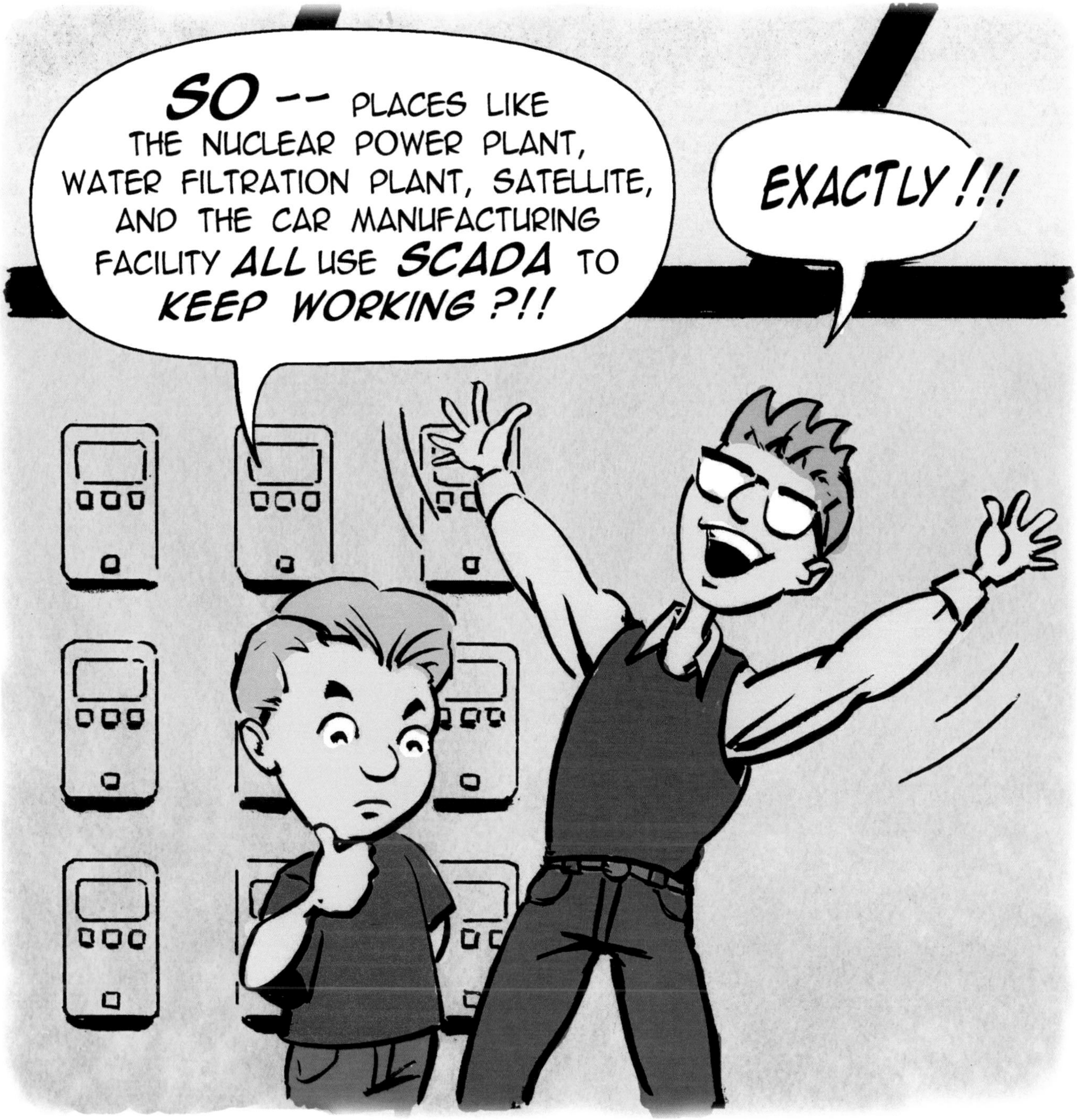
SO -- PLACES LIKE THE NUCLEAR POWER PLANT, WATER FILTRATION PLANT, SATELLITE, AND THE CAR MANUFACTURING FACILITY ALL USE SCADA TO KEEP WORKING ?!!
EXACTLY !!!

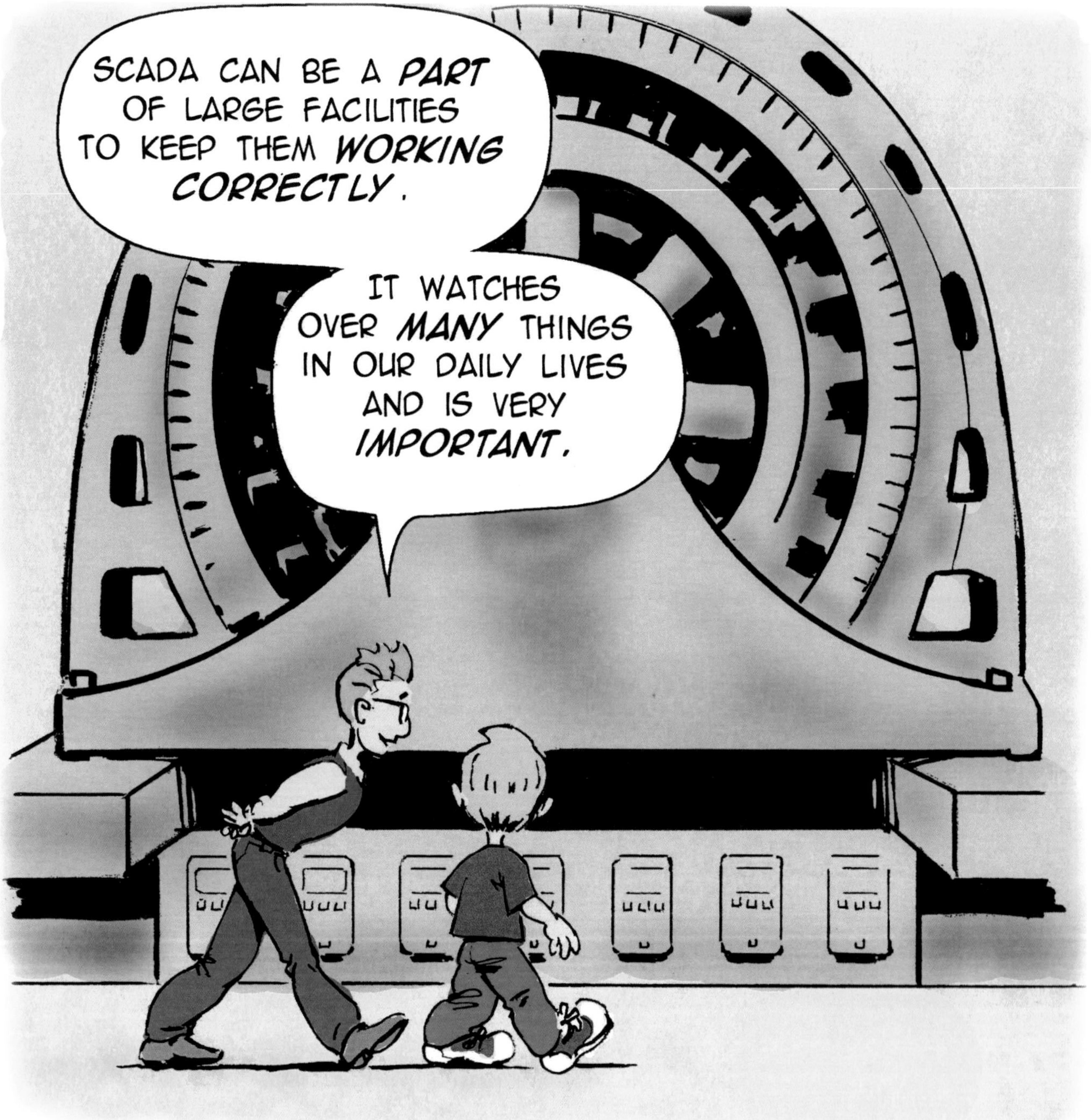
SCADA CAN BE A PART OF LARGE FACILITIES TO KEEP THEM WORKING CORRECTLY.
IT WATCHES OVER MANY THINGS IN OUR DAILY LIVES AND IS VERY IMPORTANT.

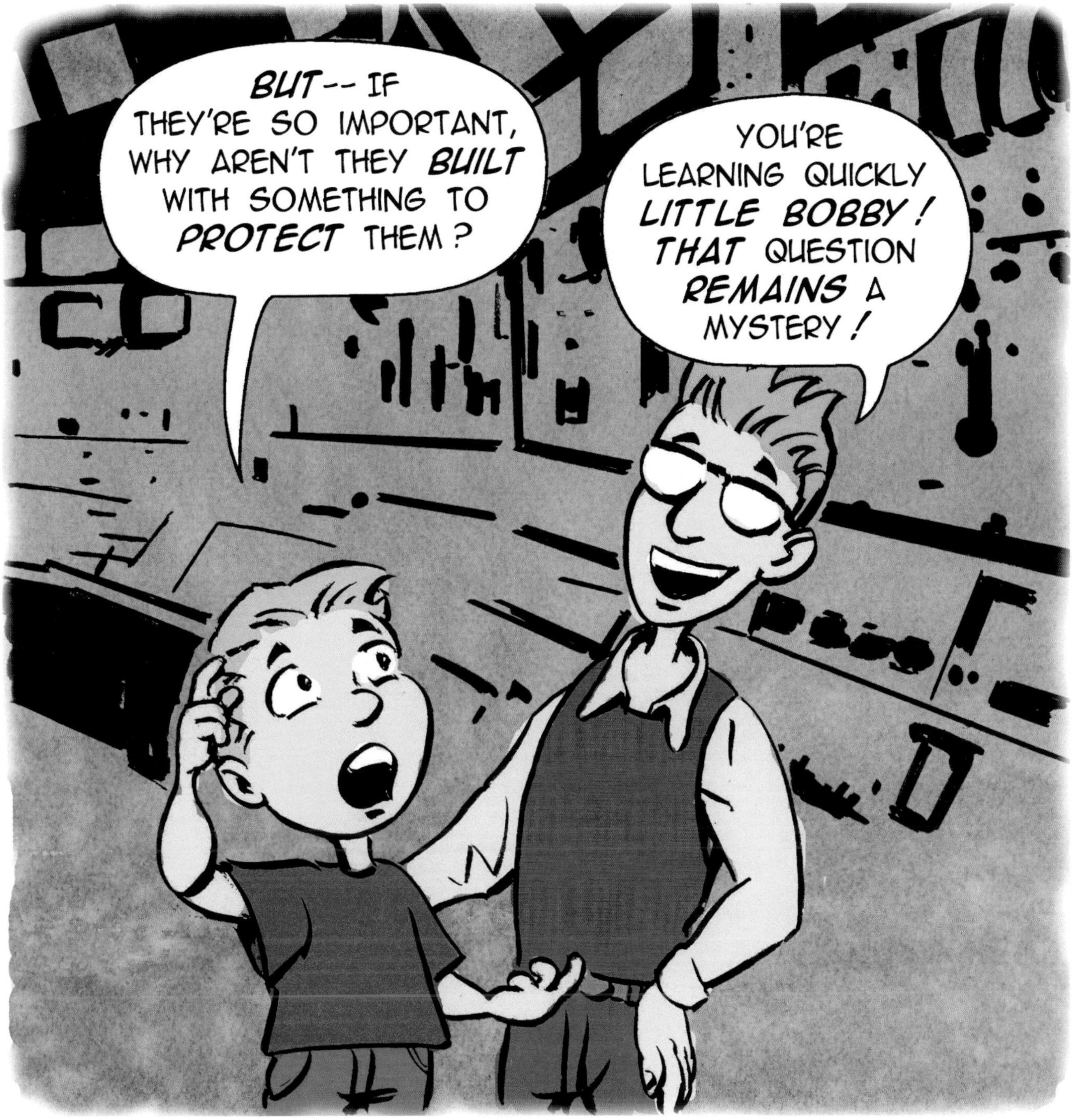
BUT-- IF THEY'RE SO IMPORTANT, WHY AREN'T THEY BUILT WITH SOMETHING TO PROTECT THEM?
YOU'RE LEARNING QUICKLY LITTLE BOBBY! THAT QUESTION REMAINS A MYSTERY!

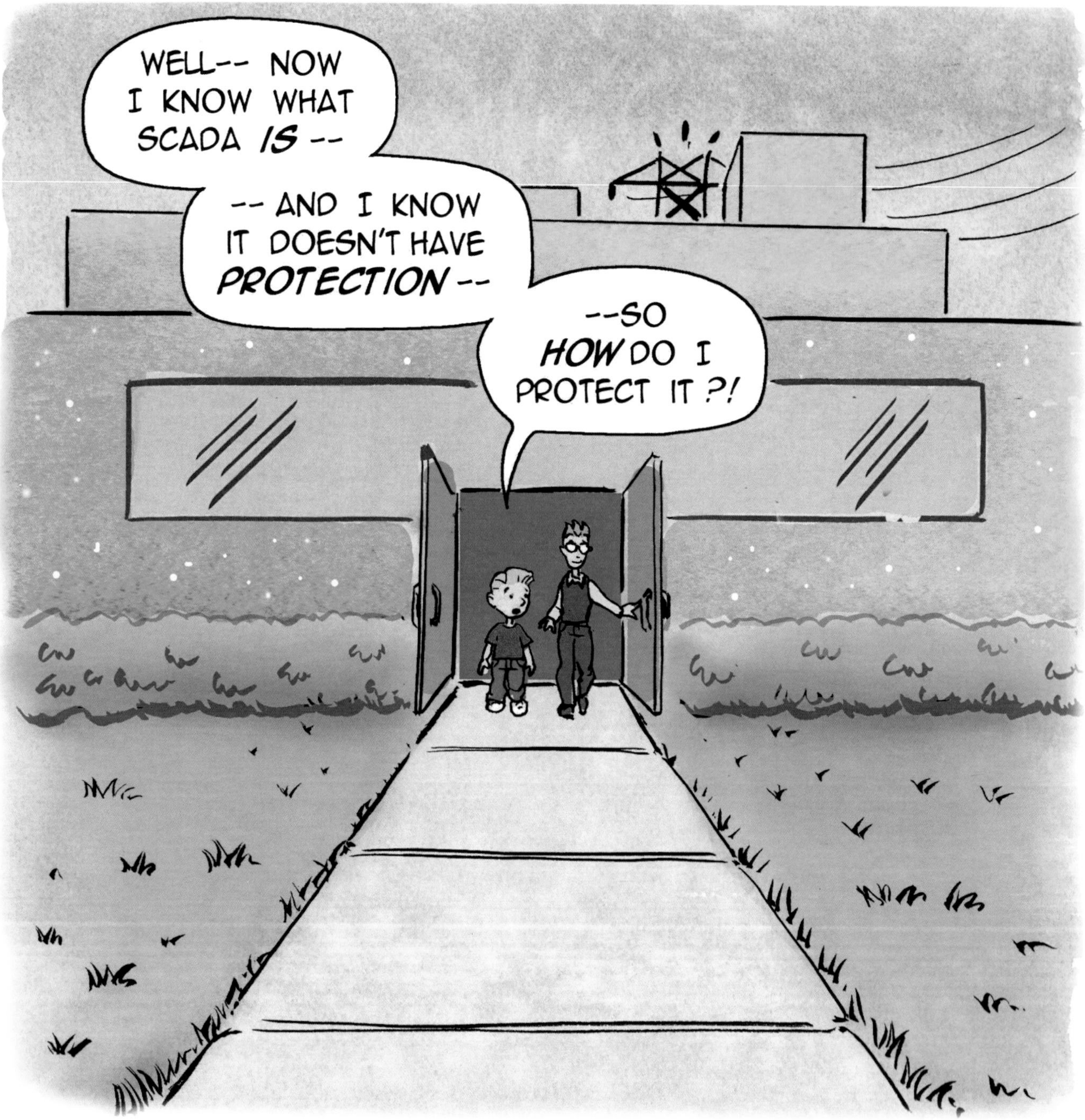
WELL-- NOW I KNOW WHAT SCADA *IS* --
-- AND I KNOW IT DOESN'T HAVE *PROTECTION* --
--SO *HOW* DO I PROTECT IT ?!

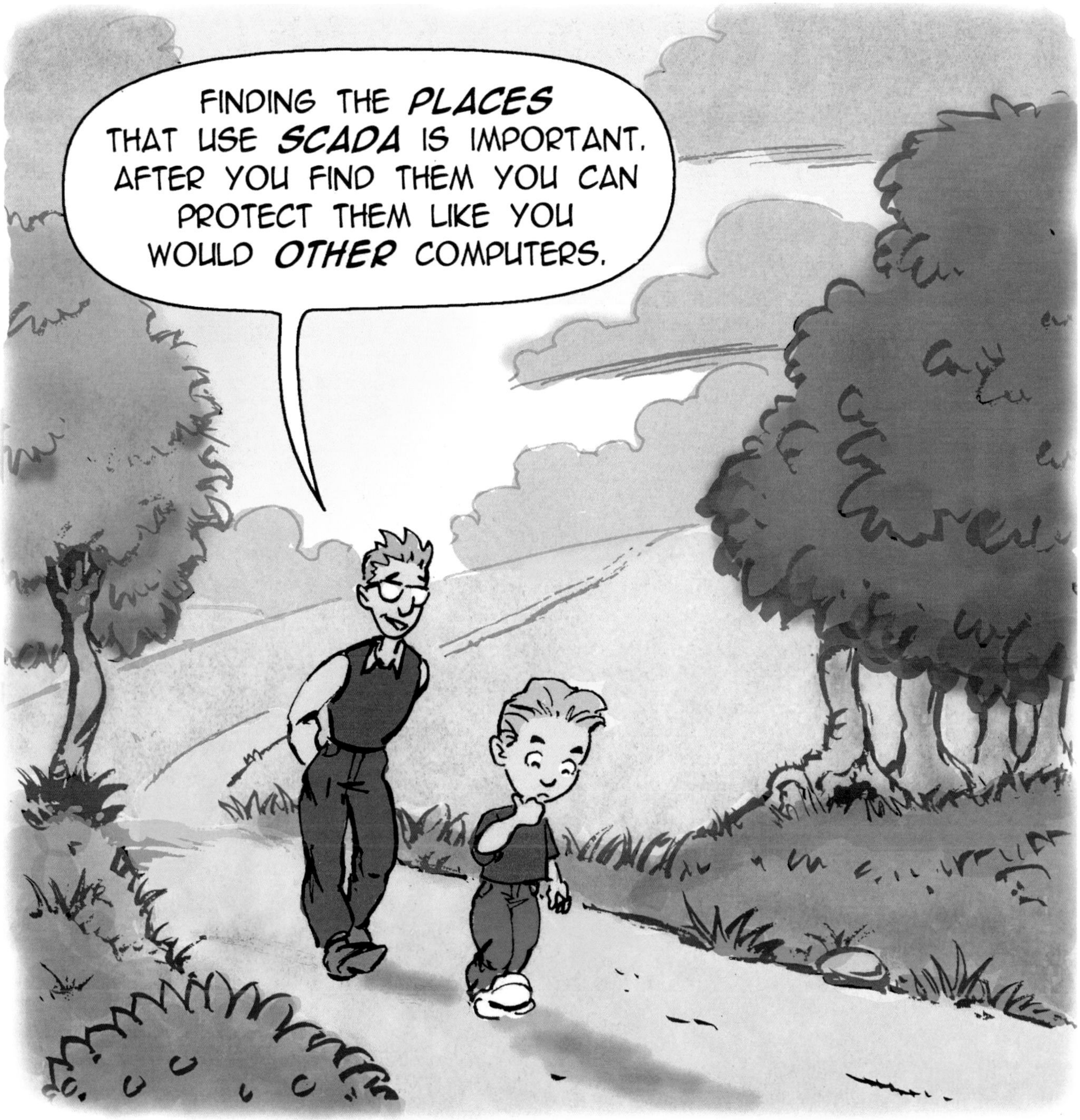
FINDING THE PLACES THAT USE SCADA IS IMPORTANT. AFTER YOU FIND THEM YOU CAN PROTECT THEM LIKE YOU WOULD OTHER COMPUTERS.

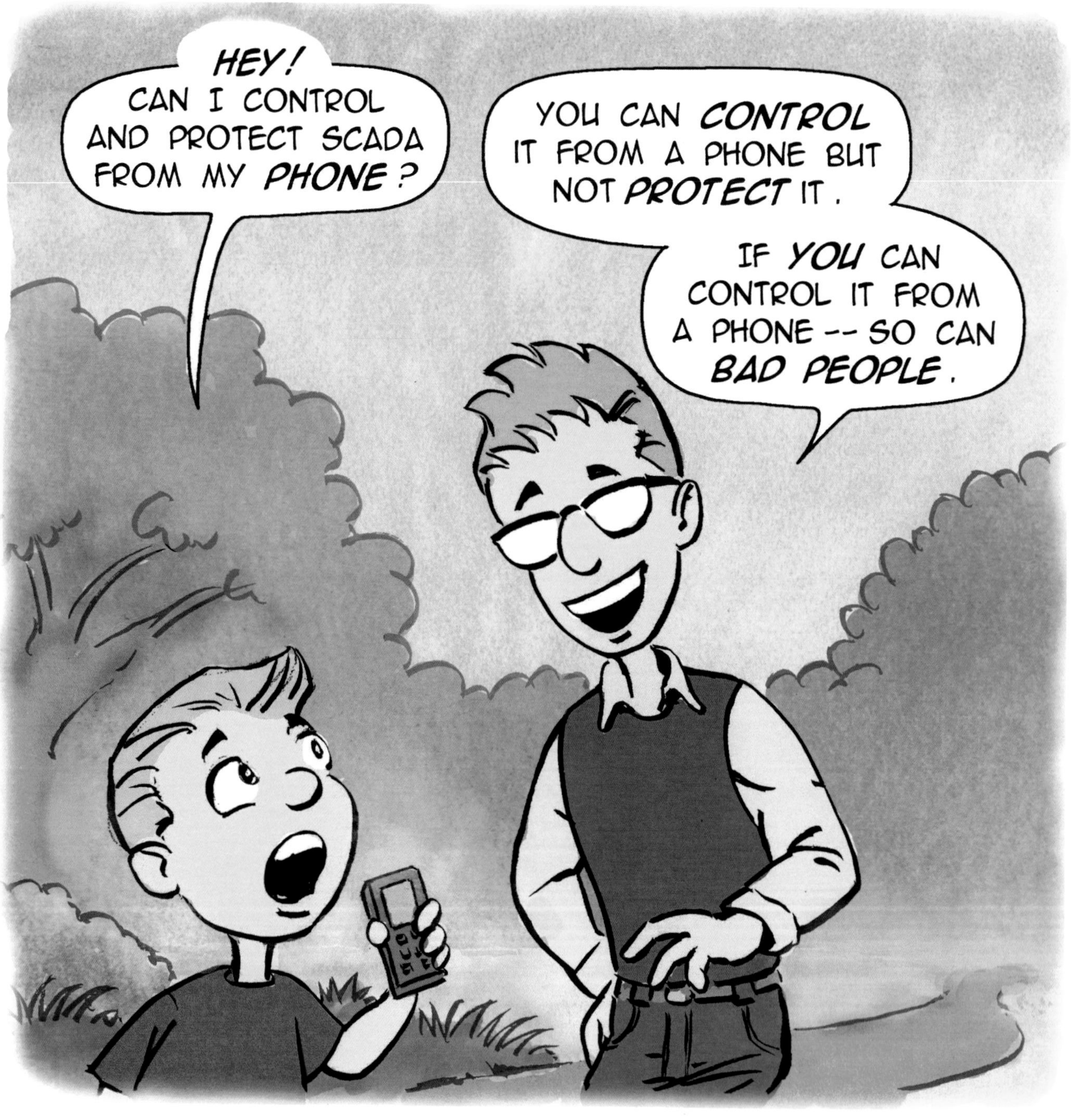
HEY! CAN I CONTROL AND PROTECT SCADA FROM MY PHONE?
YOU CAN CONTROL IT FROM A PHONE BUT NOT PROTECT IT.
IF YOU CAN CONTROL IT FROM A PHONE -- SO CAN BAD PEOPLE.

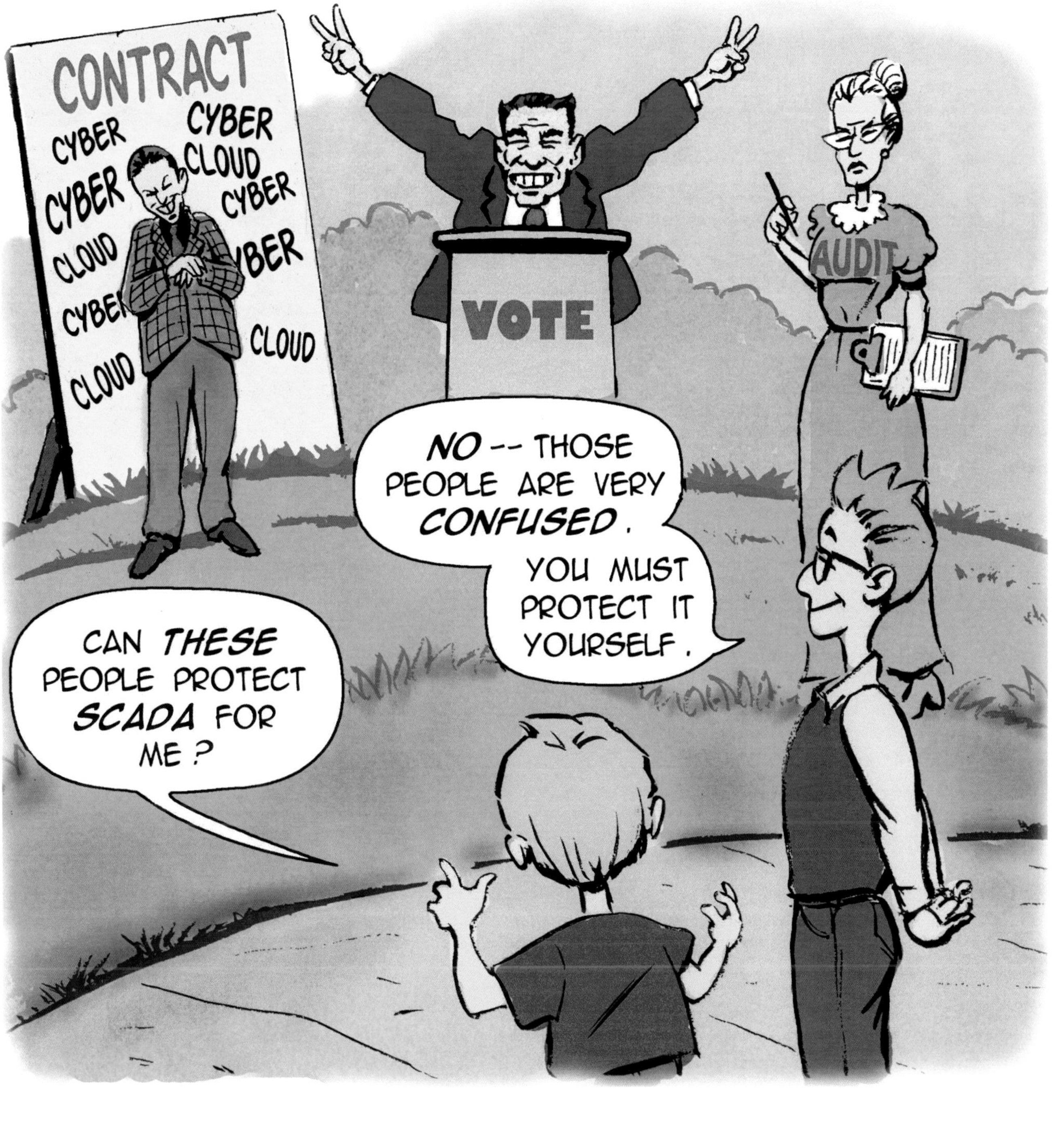
CONTRACT
CYBER
CYBER
CYBER
CLOUD
CYBER
CLOUD
CYBER
CYBER
CLOUD
CLOUD
VOTE
AUDIT
NO -- THOSE PEOPLE ARE VERY CONFUSED.
YOU MUST PROTECT IT YOURSELF.
CAN THESE PEOPLE PROTECT SCADA FOR ME?

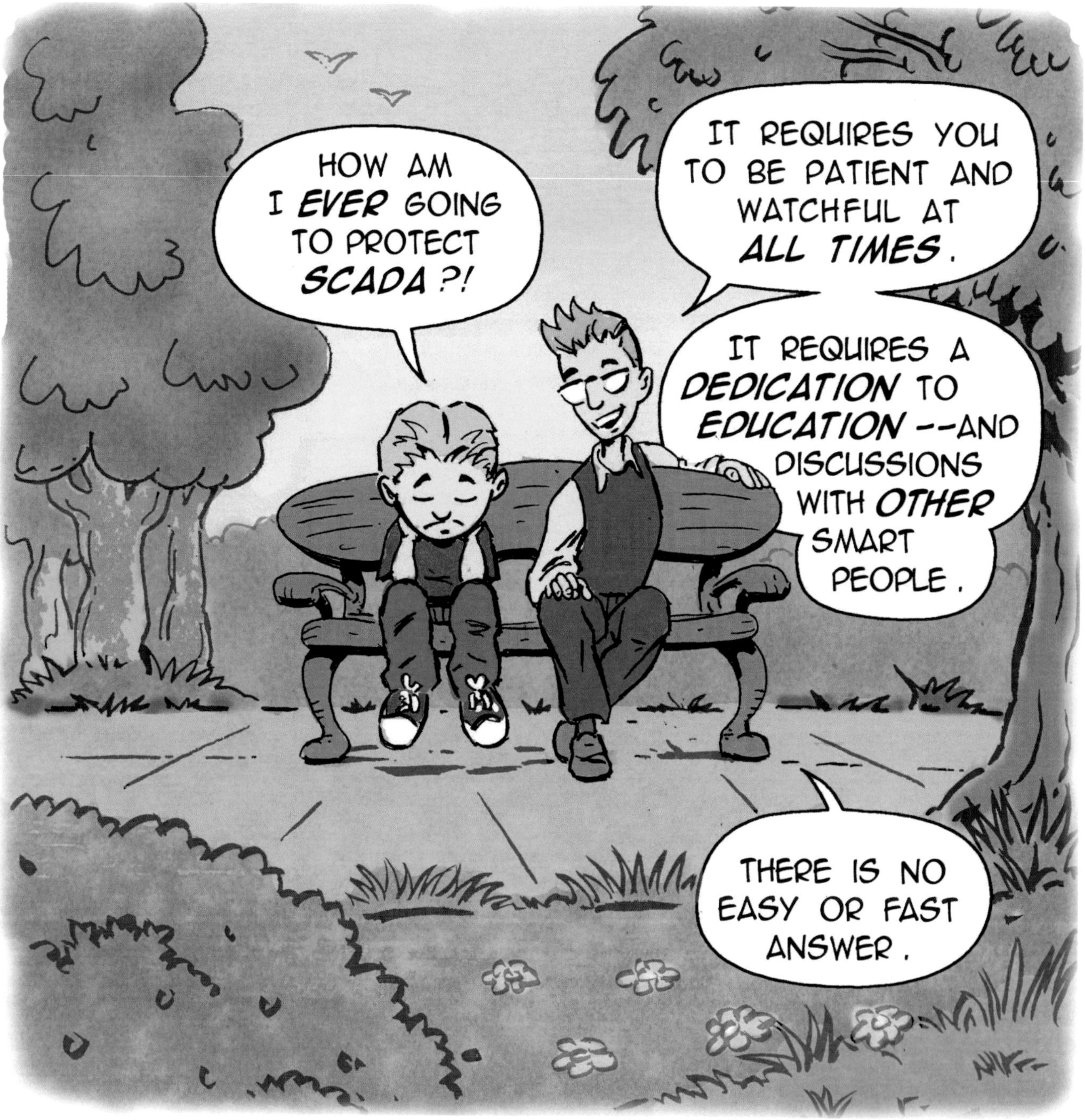
HOW AM I *EVER* GOING TO PROTECT *SCADA* ?!
IT REQUIRES YOU TO BE PATIENT AND WATCHFUL AT *ALL TIMES* .
IT REQUIRES A *DEDICATION* TO *EDUCATION* --AND DISCUSSIONS WITH *OTHER* SMART PEOPLE .
THERE IS NO EASY OR FAST ANSWER .

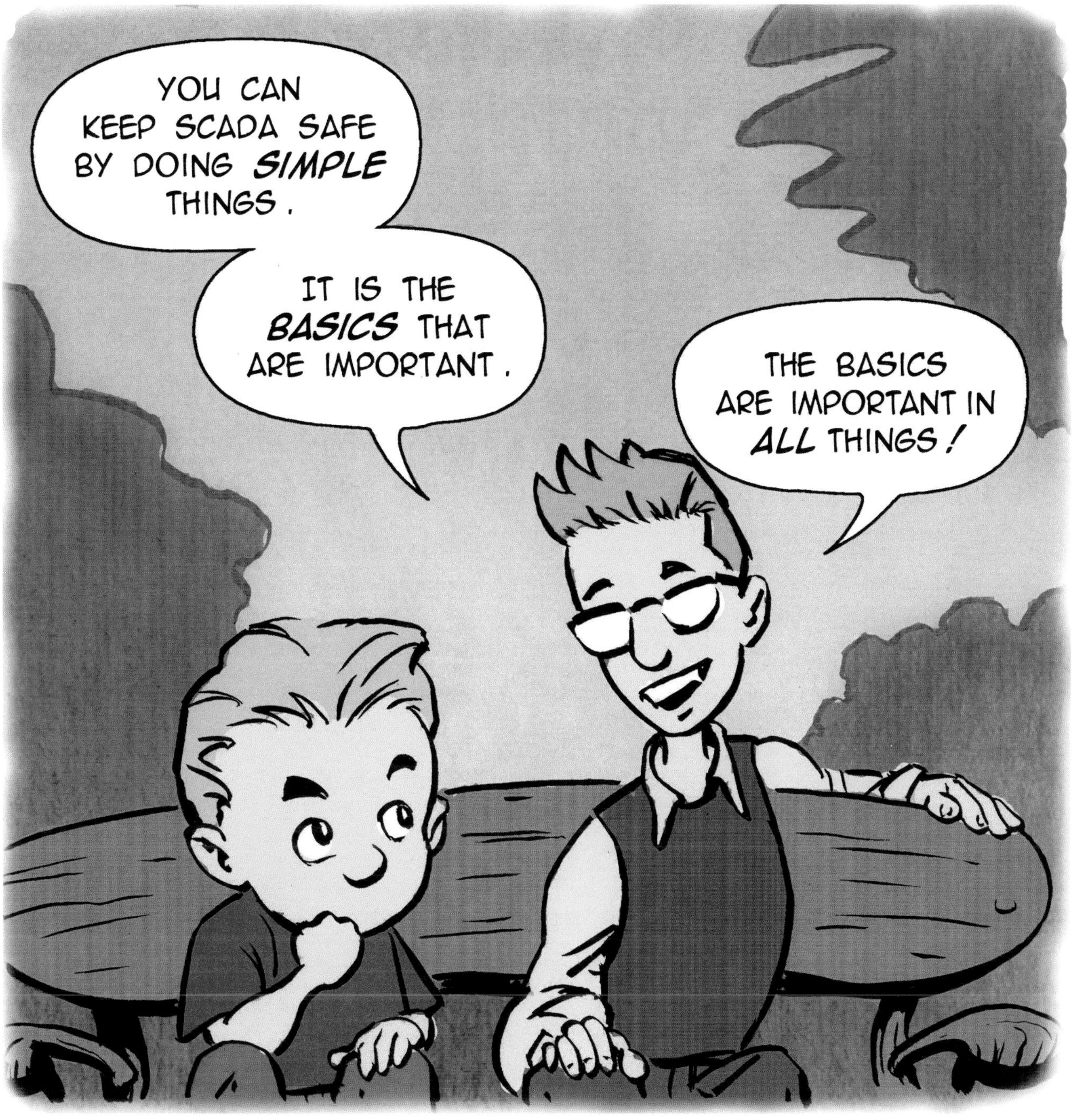
YOU CAN KEEP SCADA SAFE BY DOING SIMPLE THINGS.
IT IS THE BASICS THAT ARE IMPORTANT.
THE BASICS ARE IMPORTANT IN ALL THINGS!

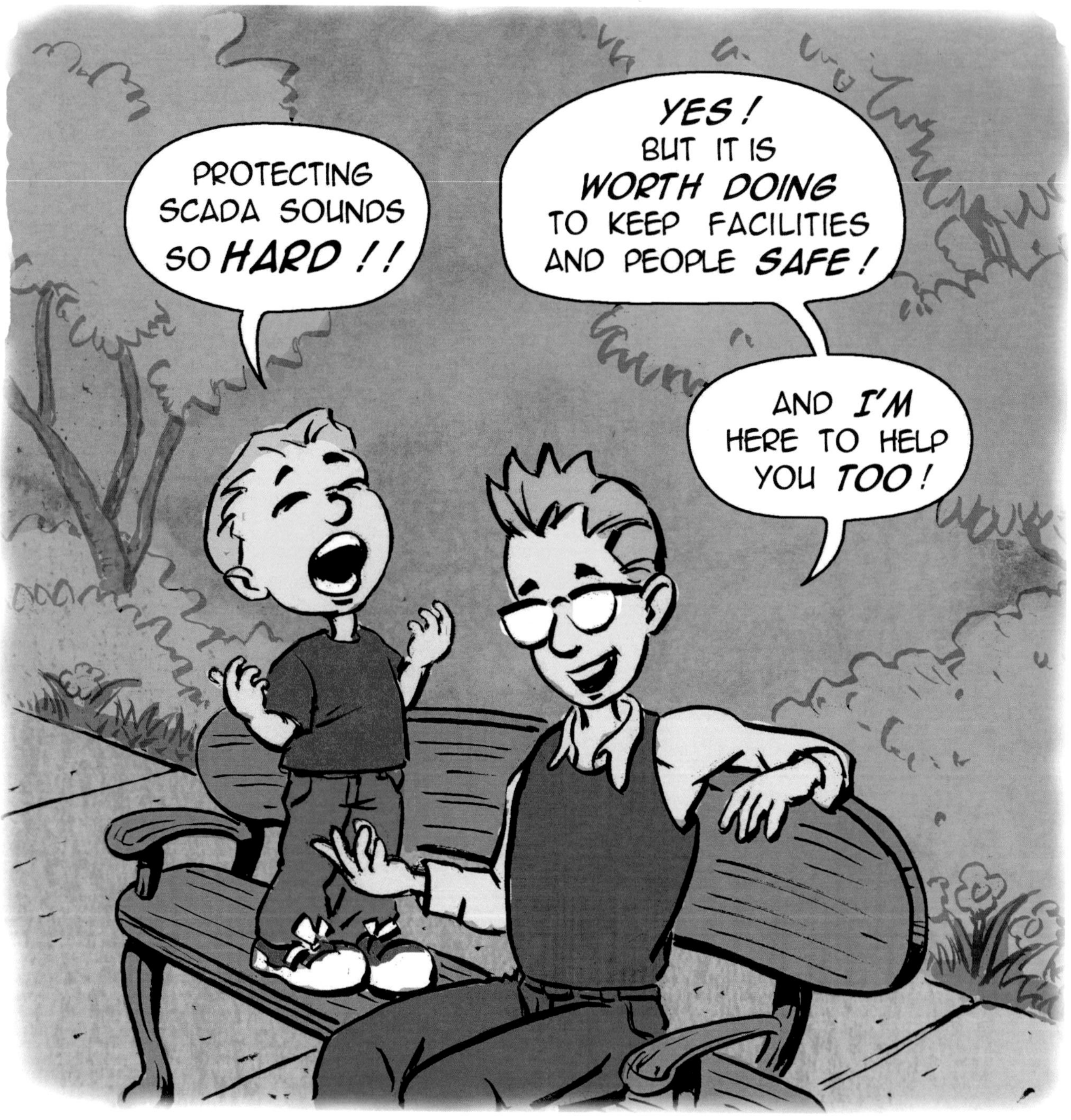
PROTECTING SCADA SOUNDS SO HARD !!
YES! BUT IT IS WORTH DOING TO KEEP FACILITIES AND PEOPLE SAFE!
AND I'M HERE TO HELP YOU TOO!

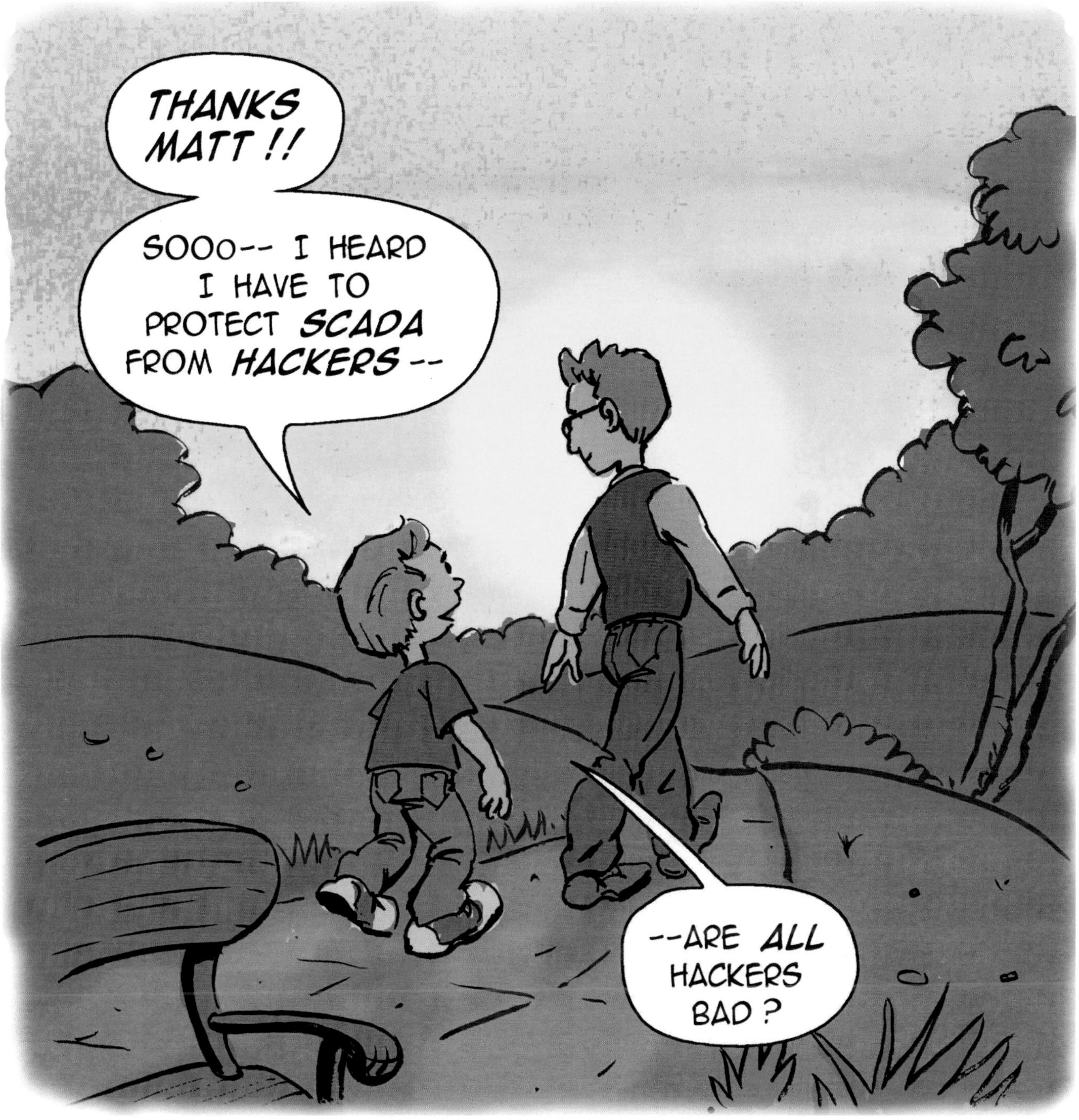
THANKS MATT !!
SOOo-- I HEARD I HAVE TO PROTECT SCADA FROM HACKERS --
--ARE ALL HACKERS BAD ?

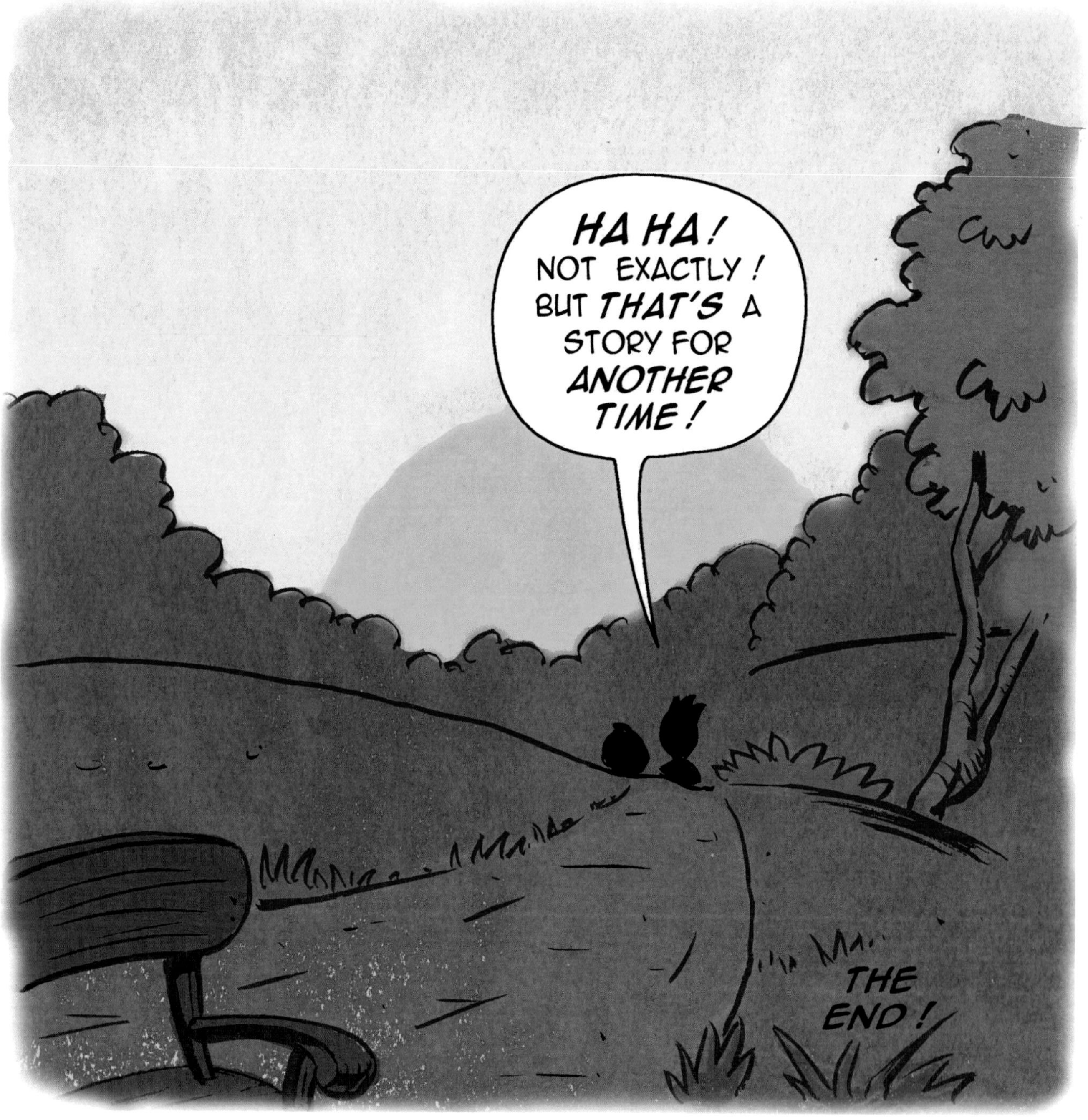
HA HA! NOT EXACTLY! BUT THAT'S A STORY FOR ANOTHER TIME!
THE END!

For information on this book, upcoming events, and more, please visit the website at: www.SCADAandMe.com

Author: Robert M. Lee

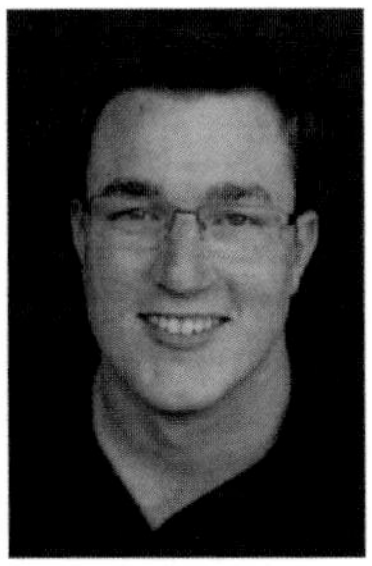

Robert M. Lee is a U.S. Air Force Cyberspace Operations Officer, Adjunct Professor at Utica College, and Director and Founder of the non-profit educational organization hackINT. He is currently pursuing a PhD in War Studies at Kings College London with research in control systems cybersecurity. He has presented at numerous international conferences and has published articles in global publications on the topics of control system cybersecurity, the future of cyberspace, and advanced digital threats. Robert is a lifelong student and educator passionate about the cyberspace domain.

Illustrator: Jeff Haas

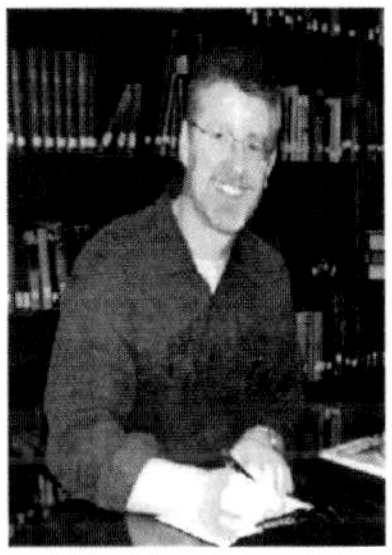

Artist and Illustrator Jeff Haas has a career that has spanned a variety of media-- from comics, book and magazine illustrations to corporate and private murals, theatrical posters and paintings. Jeff and his wife live in Michigan, where they have been remodeling a 100 year old home "forever".

You can see more of his work at *jeffhaas.daportfolio.com*